PROMPT ENGINEERING FOR EDUCATORS

DR DHEERAJ MEHROTRA

Contents

PREFACE

*Welcome to **"Prompt Engineering for Educators"** — a comprehensive guide designed to empower educators with the skills and knowledge to craft compelling prompts for diverse educational contexts. In the dynamic landscape of education, the art of prompt engineering plays a pivotal role in shaping engaging learning experiences, fostering critical thinking, and guiding students toward meaningful outcomes.*

This book delves into the multifaceted world of prompt engineering, offering educators practical insights, strategies, and examples to master the craft. Whether you are a seasoned educator looking to refine your prompt design skills or a novice seeking guidance on creating impactful learning experiences, this book is tailored to meet your needs.

Key Features of the Book:

Understanding the Art of Effective Prompts:

Explore the fundamental principles of crafting clear, concise, and purposeful prompts that resonate with learners. Understand the psychology behind prompts and their impact on student engagement.

Aligning Prompts with Learning Objectives:

Learn how to strategically align prompts with learning objectives, ensuring that each task contributes meaningfully to the educational journey. Discover techniques for seamlessly integrating prompts into curricular frameworks.

Diverse Prompt Formats for Varied Learning Styles:

Dive into various prompt formats, including written, visual, multimedia, and interactive. Tailor your approach to cater to the various learning styles of your students.

Promoting Critical Thinking through Prompts:

Uncover strategies to design prompts beyond surface-level recall, fostering critical thinking, analysis, and synthesis. Encourage students to become active participants in their own learning journey.

Adapting to Technological Advances:

Embrace the integration of technology in prompt engineering. Explore how digital tools, multimedia elements, and interactive platforms can elevate the effectiveness of your prompts in the modern classroom.

Building a Collaborative Learning Environment:

Discover the power of prompts in fostering collaboration among students. Learn how to design prompts encouraging teamwork, discussion, and shared knowledge exploration.

Providing Constructive Feedback:

Master the art of providing constructive and timely feedback on student responses. Understand how feedback loops contribute to ongoing student development and enhance the learning experience.

Continuous Improvement and Iteration:

Cultivate a mindset of continuous improvement in prompt engineering. Explore ways to gather feedback, reflect on the effectiveness of prompts, and iterate your approach for optimal impact.

This book provides practical examples, case studies, and actionable tips to enhance your prompt engineering skills. Whether you teach in a traditional classroom, engage with students online, or facilitate hybrid learning environments, the principles explored in this book are adaptable to various educational settings.

As educators, our mission is to inspire, guide, and empower the next generation. "Prompt Engineering for Educators" equips you with the tools to create meaningful and transformative learning experiences through the artful crafting of prompts.

Embark on this journey with enthusiasm, curiosity, and a commitment to excellence in education. May your prompts spark the flames of curiosity and ignite the joy of learning in the hearts of your students.

Happy prompting!

I

Understanding the Art of Effective Prompts

Prompt engineering for educators is a valuable practice that involves designing thought-provoking and stimulating prompts for discussions, reflections, and activities in educational settings.

The importance of prompt engineering for educators lies in its ability to:

Stimulate Critical Thinking:

Well-crafted prompts encourage educators to think critically about their teaching methods, classroom activities and approaches to engaging students. They prompt educators to analyze, evaluate, and reflect on their practices.

Inspire Professional Development:

Engaging prompts can inspire educators to pursue continuous professional development. They encourage teachers to seek new ideas, explore innovative teaching methods, and stay updated on the latest trends in education.

Foster Collaboration:

Prompts designed for collaboration promote discussions among educators, enabling them to share experiences, insights, and best practices. This collaborative environment contributes to a supportive professional community.

Encourage Reflection:

Reflective prompts prompt educators to analyze their teaching strategies, assess the effectiveness of lessons, and consider how to enhance student learning. Reflection is a key component of ongoing professional growth.

Enhance Creativity in Teaching:

Prompts that stimulate creativity encourage educators to think outside the box. They inspire the development of innovative teaching methods, lesson plans, and activities that capture students' interest and curiosity.

Support Student-Centric Approaches:

Student-focused prompts help educators consider the needs and perspectives of their students. This leads to the creation of learning experiences that are tailored to meet students where they are and foster a positive and inclusive classroom environment.

Integrate Interdisciplinary Approaches:

Prompts designed to encourage interdisciplinary thinking prompt educators to explore connections between different subjects and integrate diverse perspectives. This holistic approach enriches the learning experience for students.

Address Current Educational Challenges:

Thoughtful prompts can prompt educators to address current challenges in education, whether related to technology integration, diverse learning styles, or adapting to changing educational landscapes.

Promote Lifelong Learning:

Engaging prompts foster a culture of lifelong learning among educators. They emphasize the importance of staying curious, exploring new ideas, and continuously seeking ways to improve teaching practices.

Increase Motivation and Engagement:

Well-crafted prompts can inspire educators, reigniting their passion for teaching and fostering a sense of purpose. This motivation positively influences classroom dynamics and student engagement.

In summary, prompt engineering for educators is essential for creating a dynamic and responsive educational environment. It plays a key role in promoting continuous improvement, collaboration, and innovation in teaching practices, ultimately benefiting both educators and their students.

II
Aligning Prompts with Learning Objectives

Integrating a chatbot into education through prompt engineering can enhance the learning experience by providing personalized support, facilitating communication, and offering quick access to information. Here's a guide on how educators can use chatbots with prompt engineering:

1. Identify Educational Goals:

Determine the specific educational goals the chatbot will address. This could include providing information, answering common questions, offering learning resources, or assisting with administrative tasks.

2. Define User Personas:

Identify the target audience for the chatbot, such as students, parents, or educators. Tailor prompts to the needs and preferences of each user persona.

3. Design Natural Language Prompts:

Create natural language prompts that users are likely to use when interacting with the chatbot. Consider common questions, concerns, or topics relevant to the educational context.

4. Personalization and Adaptive Learning:

Use prompt engineering to personalize the chatbot's responses based on user interactions. Adapt to individual learning preferences, progress, and challenges.

5. Information Retrieval:

Structure prompts to retrieve relevant information quickly. For instance, a prompt like "Find resources on [topic]" can direct the chatbot to provide links, documents, or other learning materials.

6. Problem-Solving and Critical Thinking Prompts:

Include prompts that encourage problem-solving and critical thinking. For example, "How would you solve [educational challenge]?" can prompt users to think critically about educational issues.

7. Feedback and Assessment:

Use chatbots to collect feedback on educational experiences. Create prompts for users to share their thoughts on lessons, activities, or the overall learning environment.

8. Integration with Learning Platforms:

If applicable, integrate the chatbot with learning management systems or educational platforms. Create prompts that streamline access to course materials, announcements, and assignments.

9. Language Learning Support:

Develop prompts for language learners, including vocabulary practice, grammar explanations, and conversational interactions to reinforce language skills.

10. Study Aid and Revision:

- Create prompts that assist students in their studies, such as providing flashcards, summarizing concepts, or offering quiz questions for revision.

11. Time Management and Reminders:

- Design prompts for time management, reminders for assignments, upcoming exams, or important events. Encourage students to set study goals and create reminders.

12. Student Support Services:

- Incorporate prompts related to student support services, such as counseling, academic advising, or career guidance. Ensure the chatbot can direct users to the appropriate resources.

13. Professional Development for Educators:

- Develop prompts that support educators in their professional development. Provide resources, workshop information, and opportunities for collaboration.

14. Accessibility and Inclusivity:

- Use prompts to ensure the chatbot is accessible and inclusive. Include features like text-to-speech, multilingual support, and options for users with diverse needs.

15. Continuous Improvement:

- Establish a feedback loop to continuously improve the chatbot. Encourage users to provide feedback on prompts, user experience, and additional features they would find beneficial.

16. Privacy and Security Prompts:

- Include prompts that address privacy and security concerns. Communicate how user data is handled, ensuring compliance with data protection regulations.

17. Collaboration and Community Building:

- Facilitate prompts that encourage collaboration and community building. For instance, prompts related to group projects, study groups, or discussion forums.

18. Integration with Chat Platforms:

- Consider integrating the chatbot with popular messaging platforms used by students, making it easily accessible and *convenient.*

19. Gamification Elements:

- Infuse prompts with gamification elements to enhance engagement. For example, create prompts for educational quizzes, challenges, or interactive learning games.

20. Monitoring and Analytics:

- Implement prompts that allow educators to monitor and analyze chatbot interactions. Gather insights on user engagement, popular queries, and areas for improvement.

By strategically employing prompt engineering, educators can harness the potential of chatbots to support and enhance the educational experience for both students and educators. Regularly assess the effectiveness of prompts and make adjustments to optimize the chatbot's performance continually.

III

Common Prompts in Use for Best Results on ChatGPT

Using clear and specific prompts that provide context and direction helps achieve the best results when interacting with ChatGPT.

Here are some common types of prompts that tend to yield effective results:

Questions: Ask straightforward, concise, and specific questions. Provide enough context to help ChatGPT understand what you're asking and what response you expect.

Example: "Can you explain the concept of quantum entanglement in simple terms?"

Requests for Information: Request information on a particular topic, providing relevant details to guide ChatGPT's response.

Example: "Please provide an overview of the causes and effects of climate change."

Problem Statements: Describe a problem or challenge you're facing and ask for advice, solutions, or insights.

Example: "I'm struggling to stay focused while working from home. Any tips for improving productivity?"

Creative Prompts: Encourage creativity by providing an open-ended prompt or asking for imaginative responses.

Example: "Imagine a world where humans can teleport. What do you think would be the biggest challenges and benefits?"

Opinion Questions: Seek ChatGPT's opinion or perspective on a topic, encouraging thoughtful responses.

Example: "What do you think are the most promising areas for technological innovation in the next decade?"

Scenario-Based Questions: Present a hypothetical scenario and ask ChatGPT to respond or provide insights based on that scenario.

Example: "You're planning a trip to Japan and want to experience the local culture. What activities would you recommend?"

Summarization Requests: Ask ChatGPT to summarize a text, a news article, or a complex concept.

Example: "Can you summarize the main findings of the recent study on the effects of social media on mental health?"

Teaching or Explanation Requests: Request ChatGPT to teach or explain a topic, concept, or process in detail.

Example: "Could you provide a step-by-step guide to setting up a personal budget?"

Using these prompts effectively allows you to guide ChatGPT in providing more relevant, accurate, and helpful responses tailored to your needs and interests.

IV
Diverse Prompt Formats for Varied Learning Styles

Here are examples of prompts that educators can use for chatbots in various educational contexts:

1. General Information:

Prompt: "Tell me about upcoming school events."

Response: The chatbot details upcoming events, including dates, times, and locations.

2. Course Information:

Prompt: "What topics will we cover in this week's lessons?"

Response: The chatbot outlines the topics, assignments, and resources for the current week's lessons.

3. Assignment Help:

Prompt: "I need help with my assignment on [topic]."

Response: The chatbot offers assistance, resources, tips, or clarification on the assignment.

4. Study Resources:

Prompt: "Recommend study materials for [subject]."

Response: The chatbot suggests relevant textbooks, online resources, or study guides for the specified subject.

5. Language Learning:

Prompt: "Help me practice [language] vocabulary."

Response: The chatbot presents vocabulary flashcards and engages in interactive language practice.

6. Feedback Collection:

Prompt: "Share your thoughts on today's class."

Response: The chatbot collects feedback on the lesson, encouraging students to provide comments and suggestions.

7. Library Resources:

Prompt: "Find books on [topic] in the library."

Response: The chatbot provides a list of books related to the specified topic in the library.

8. Exam Preparation:

Prompt: "Give me tips for preparing for exams."

Response: The chatbot offers strategies for adequate exam preparation, time management, and stress reduction.

9. Career Guidance:

Prompt: "Explore careers in [field]."

Response: The chatbot shares information about potential careers, required skills, and educational pathways in the specified field.

10. Technology Support:

*- *Prompt:* "Help me troubleshoot issues with my online learning platform." - *Response:* The chatbot provides step-by-step troubleshooting guidance or directs the user to technical support.*

11. Parent-Teacher Meeting:

*- *Prompt:* "Tell me about the upcoming parent-teacher meeting." - *Response:* The chatbot details the schedule, agenda, and how parents can participate.*

12. Extracurricular Activities:

*- *Prompt:* "What extracurricular activities are available?" - *Response:* The chatbot lists available clubs, sports, activities, meeting times, and locations.*

13. Accessibility Information:

- *Prompt:* "How can I access learning materials in an accessible format?" - *Response:* The chatbot provides information on accessible formats and support services for students with diverse needs.

14. Community Engagement:

- *Prompt:* "How can I get involved in community service projects?" - *Response:* The chatbot offers information on available community service opportunities and how to participate.

15. Professional Development:

- *Prompt:* "Find workshops for professional development."
- *Response:* The chatbot provides a list of upcoming workshops, conferences, and training sessions for educators.

16. Virtual Classroom Access:

- *Prompt:* "Connect me to the virtual classroom for today's lesson." - *Response:* The chatbot provides a direct link or instructions for accessing the virtual classroom platform.

17. Well-Being Tips:

- *Prompt:* "Share tips for maintaining mental well-being."
- *Response:* The chatbot offers tips on stress management, self-care, and maintaining a healthy work-life balance.

18. Homework Reminders:

- *Prompt:* "Remind me about my homework deadlines." - *Response:* The chatbot sends reminders for upcoming homework assignments, including due dates and requirements.

19. Group Project Collaboration:

- *Prompt:* "Help me coordinate with my group for the project." - *Response:* The chatbot facilitates communication, scheduling, and collaboration among group members.

20. Motivational Quotes:

- *Prompt:* "Inspire me with a motivational quote." - *Response:* The chatbot shares a motivational quote to encourage positivity and motivation.

These examples demonstrate the versatility of chatbots in addressing a wide range of educational needs. Educators can customize and expand upon these prompts based on their specific requirements and their students' preferences.

V
5 S Model of Prompt Creation

The Five S model of Prompt Creation is a structured approach emphasising key principles for developing effective prompts. Each "S" represents a critical aspect of prompt creation. Let's explore the Five S model:

1. Specific:

Definition: Ensure that prompts are clear, concise, and specific in their intent. Avoid ambiguity to prevent misunderstandings.

Example: "Describe the main events of World War II" is specific, whereas "Discuss history" is vague.

2. Strategic:

Definition: Develop prompts strategically to align with learning objectives, encourage critical thinking, and guide students toward desired outcomes.

Example: Instead of "What is the capital of France?" use "Explain the historical and cultural significance of Paris as the capital of France."

3. Structured:

Definition: Organize prompts logically and coherently. Provide a clear framework for responses to enhance understanding.

Example: Use a step-by-step prompt like "Identify, analyze, and compare the key themes in two assigned readings."

4. Supportive:

Definition: Ensure prompts are supportive of diverse learning styles and abilities. Offer guidance, resources, or examples to assist learners.

Example: "Compose a poem inspired by [literary work] using at least three literary devices. Refer to the attached guide for examples."

5. Scaffolded:

Definition: Scaffold prompts by gradually increasing complexity. Start with foundational questions and progressively move to more advanced ones.

Example: "Define a simple machine" and progress to "Illustrate how a complex machine employs the principles of simple machines."

Adhering to the Five S model, educators can create prompts tailored to their instructional goals, support diverse learners, and foster critical thinking and engagement. This model provides a systematic approach to prompt development, enhancing the overall effectiveness of educational interactions.

1. Specific:

Unclear Prompt: "Discuss the topic."

Specific Prompt: "Explain the impact of climate change on marine ecosystems, considering factors such as rising sea levels and ocean acidification."

2. Strategic:

Non-Strategic Prompt: "What is the capital of Italy?"

Strategic Prompt: "Evaluate the historical and cultural significance of Rome as the capital of Italy, considering its role in art, architecture, and political history."

3. Structured:

Unstructured Prompt: "Write about your favourite book."

Structured Prompt: "Compose a literary analysis of your favourite book, addressing themes, character development, and the author's writing style."

4. Supportive:

Unsupportive Prompt: "Explain the scientific method."

Supportive Prompt: "Describe the steps of the scientific method and refer to the attached infographic for visual representation and examples."

5. Scaffolded:

Non-Scaffolded Prompt: "Discuss the causes of the American Revolution."

Scaffolded Prompt:

Level 1: "Identify three causes of the American Revolution."

Level 2: "Explain the economic factors that contributed to the tensions leading to the American Revolution."

Level 3: "Evaluate the role of key individuals in the American Revolution, analyzing their impact on the course of history."

These examples illustrate how applying the Five S model can transform generic prompts into more specific, strategic, structured, supportive, and scaffolded versions, enhancing their effectiveness in guiding learning and assessment.

VI
Structuring the Outputs for Chatbots

Structuring the outputs for chatbots involves designing responses that are informative, engaging, and aligned with educational goals. Educators can use prompts strategically to guide the chatbot's outputs. Here's a guide on structuring chatbot outputs using prompts:

1. Align Outputs with Learning Objectives:

Prompt: "Provide information on [topic]."

Output Structure: Present information in a structured manner, covering key concepts, examples, and relevant details. Align the output with specific learning objectives.

2. Encourage Critical Thinking:

Prompt: "Discuss the implications of [concept]."

Output Structure: Encourage critical thinking by presenting multiple perspectives, prompting analysis, and asking follow-up questions to stimulate further reflection.

3. Offer Resources and References:

Prompt: "Recommend resources for [subject]."

Output Structure: Provide a list of recommended readings, online resources, or multimedia content. Include brief descriptions to guide learners in choosing relevant materials.

4. Interactive Learning:

Prompt: "Engage in a quiz on [topic]."

Output Structure: Create an interactive output with quiz questions, immediate feedback, and explanations for correct answers. Enhance engagement through gamification elements.

5. Supportive Feedback:

Prompt: "Review my essay on [topic]."

Output Structure: Offer constructive feedback, pointing out strengths and areas for improvement. Include suggestions for further research or refining arguments.

6. Problem-Solving Scenarios:

Prompt: "Solve a problem related to [subject]."

Output Structure: Present a real-world problem, guide users through the problem-solving process, and provide feedback on the steps taken. Encourage application of knowledge.

7. Step-by-Step Guidance:

Prompt: "Explain the process of [procedure]."

Output Structure: Break down the procedure into clear steps, providing detailed explanations, visual aids, and tips to ensure a comprehensive understanding.

8. Peer Collaboration:

Prompt: "Connect me with peers interested in [topic]."

Output Structure: Facilitate peer collaboration by creating a discussion forum or connecting users with shared interests. Encourage knowledge-sharing and collaborative learning.

9. Time Management Tips:

Prompt: "Provide tips for effective time management."

Output Structure: Offer practical tips, time-saving strategies, and tools to enhance time management skills. Include examples relevant to educational tasks.

10. Personalized Learning Paths:

vbnetCopy code

*- *Prompt:* "Recommend a personalized study plan for [subject]." - *Output Structure:* Tailor study plans based on the user's proficiency level, learning style, and goals. Provide a roadmap with suggested resources and milestones.*

11. Learning Assessments:

vbnetCopy code

- *Prompt:* "Assess my understanding of [concept]." - *Output Structure:* Create quizzes or assessments that gauge the user's comprehension. Offer detailed feedback and direct users to additional resources for areas of improvement.

12. Visualizations and Infographics:

markdownCopy code

- *Prompt:* "Explain [complex concept] visually." - *Output Structure:* Use visualizations, infographics, or diagrams to simplify complex concepts. Reinforce visual learning through clear and engaging graphics.

13. Motivational Messages:

vbnetCopy code

- *Prompt:* "Share a motivational message for studying." - *Output Structure:* Provide inspirational quotes, success stories, or encouragement tailored to the user's educational journey. Reinforce a positive mindset.

14. Reflection and Journaling:

markdownCopy code

- *Prompt:* "Guide me in reflecting on [learning experience]."
- *Output Structure:* Facilitate reflection by asking guiding questions. Encourage users to journal their thoughts, insights, and areas for growth.

15. Multimodal Outputs:

vbnetCopy code

- *Prompt:* "Teach me about [historical event]." - *Output Structure:* Combine text with multimedia elements like images, videos, or audio clips to create a rich and immersive learning experience.

16. Inclusive Outputs:

markdownCopy code

- *Prompt:* "Provide accessible content for [diverse learners]."
- *Output Structure:* Ensure outputs are accessible to diverse learners, including alternative formats, transcripts, and options for customization.

17. Culminating Projects:

markdownCopy code

- *Prompt:* "Guide me in a culminating project for [course]."
- *Output Structure:* Offer project ideas, milestones, and resources for a culminating project. Foster creativity and application of knowledge.

18. Language Learning Support:

markdownCopy code

- *Prompt:* "Help me practice [language] speaking." - *Output Structure:* Incorporate language practice with conversation starters, pronunciation guides, and interactive dialogues.

19. Feedback on Progress:

markdownCopy code

- *Prompt:* "Assess my progress in [learning area]." - *Output Structure:* Provide a summary of user progress, highlighting achievements and suggesting areas for continued focus and improvement.

20. Continuous Improvement Suggestions:

vbnetCopy code

- *Prompt:* "How can I improve my learning experience?"
- *Output Structure:* Solicit user feedback on the chatbot's performance and suggest improvements or additional

features based on user input.

By structuring chatbot outputs strategically, educators can enhance the overall learning experience, cater to diverse needs, and foster meaningful engagement with educational content. The key is to align the outputs with pedagogical goals and create a supportive and interactive learning environment.

You

VII
Improving Prompts as Educators

Improving your prompt engineering experience as an educator involves refining your skills in crafting effective and engaging prompts for various educational contexts. Here are some tips to enhance your prompt engineering experience:

1. Understand Your Audience:

Know your students' needs, interests, and learning styles. Tailor your prompts to resonate with their preferences and effectively engage them.

2. Align with Learning Objectives:

Ensure that each prompt is directly tied to specific learning objectives. This alignment helps students see the relevance of the task and promotes focused learning.

3. Use Clear and Concise Language:

Craft prompts using easy-to-understand language. Avoid unnecessary complexity and ensure clarity in conveying the task or question.

4. Provide Context:

Offer context for the prompt to help students understand its relevance. Explain why the task is essential and how it contributes to their learning experience.

5. Incorporate Real-World Applications:

Connect prompts to real-world scenarios whenever possible. This fosters a sense of relevance and helps students see the practical applications of their learning.

6. Include Diverse Formats:

Experiment with different prompt formats, including written, visual, multimedia, or interactive prompts. Catering to diverse learning styles enhances engagement.

7. Encourage Critical Thinking:

Design prompts that prompt students to think critically, analyze information, and form reasoned opinions. Encourage them to go beyond simple recall.

8. Provide Clear Guidelines:

Clearly outline the expectations and guidelines for the task. Include any specific criteria for evaluation, ensuring that students understand what is expected of them.

9. Scaffold Complex Tasks:

Break down complex tasks into smaller, manageable steps. Provide scaffolding to support students in gradually developing their skills and understanding.

10. Collect Student Input:

csharpCopy code

- Solicit feedback from students on the effectiveness of prompts. Ask for their input on clarity, relevance, and how well the prompts align with their learning needs.

11. Use Technology Thoughtfully:

rCopy code

- Leverage technology for interactive and engaging prompts. Consider incorporating multimedia elements, interactive quizzes, or collaborative tools to enhance the learning experience.

12. Promote Collaboration:

vbnetCopy code

Design prompts that encourage collaboration among students. Incorporate group activities and discussions to foster a sense of community and shared learning.

13. Emphasize Reflection:

vbnetCopy code

Include prompts that prompt students to reflect on their learning experiences. Encourage self-assessment and insight into students' learning processes.

14. Stay Open to Adaptations:

vbnetCopy code

- Be open to adapting prompts based on student feedback and evolving learning needs. Flexibility allows you to refine prompts for optimal effectiveness.

15. Model Expected Responses:

cssCopy code

- Provide model responses or examples to illustrate the type of response you are looking for. This helps clarify expectations and provides a reference point for students.

16. Connect Cross-Curricular Concepts:

vbnetCopy code

- Foster interdisciplinary connections by incorporating prompts that bridge concepts from different subject areas. This holistic approach enriches students' understanding.

17. Encourage Creativity:

rustCopy code

- *Design prompts that allow for creative expression. Encourage students to think outside the box, express their ideas uniquely, and showcase their creativity.*

18. *Offer Timely Feedback:*

csharpCopy code

- *Provide timely and constructive feedback on student responses. This helps reinforce learning and guides students in understanding areas for improvement.*

19. *Stay Informed on Educational Trends:*

csharpCopy code

- *Stay updated on current educational trends and methodologies. Incorporate innovative, prompt engineering approaches that align with the evolving landscape of education.*

20. *Reflect and Iterate:*

csharpCopy code

- Regularly reflect on the effectiveness of your prompts. Identify what works well and areas for improvement. Iteratively refine your prompt engineering skills based on ongoing experiences.

• 46

By continuously refining your prompt engineering skills and staying attuned to your students' needs and preferences, you can create a more engaging and effective learning experience in your educational setting. Experiment with various approaches, seek feedback and be open to adapting your prompts for continuous improvement.

VIII
Providing Constructive Feedback

Be Particular:

Illustrate with precise instances what was effective and what could be enhanced. Avoid imprecise statements and emphasize feedback that the engineer can implement.

Emphasize Conduct Rather Than Personality:

Construct feedback based on observable actions and behaviours instead of forming opinions about the engineer's character or demeanour. This facilitates the maintenance of an objective and professional development-oriented discourse.

Emphasize Strengths:

Commence by recognizing the engineer's merits and accomplishments. Acknowledging their contributions fosters rapport-building and establishes a constructive atmosphere for the feedback exchange.

Consider the areas that require improvement:

Determine specific domains in which the engineer may improve their proficiency or aptitude. Provide specific recommendations for enhancement and offer necessary resources or assistance to facilitate their achievement.

Convey Context and Influence:

Elucidate how the actions or behaviours of the engineer affect the organization, team, or project. Offering context facilitates their comprehension of the feedback's significance and inspires them to implement constructive modifications.

Promote Self-Reflection:

Advocate for engineers to introspect their performance and discern areas for further development. Employ open-ended inquiries to foster self-awareness and critical thinking.

Implement the "Sandwich" Method: Positive feedback should be sandwiched between constructive criticism. Commence and conclude the feedback dialogue by offering commendations and acknowledgements while addressing aspects that could be enhanced in the interim.

It is advisable to deliver feedback promptly, preferably shortly after the observed behaviour or action. Providing timely feedback enables the engineer to rectify their course and implement enhancements promptly.

Preserve a Growth Mindset: Encourage a culture of learning and continuous improvement. Highlight the notion that feedback serves as a chance for progress and advancement, not an evaluation of one's performance.

Sustained After: Consistently schedule follow-up discussions to assess progress and offer continuous support. Regularly monitor the engineer's feedback implementation and provide further direction if necessary.

By adhering to these prescribed principles, one can offer constructive criticism that bolsters timely engineering methodologies and facilitates the professional development of engineers.

IX

Importance of Prompt Engineering

There are several reasons why prompt engineering is critical, which include the following:

Prompt engineering facilitates organizations' ability to promptly address market demands, consumer feedback, and emerging trends. By prioritising quickness and agility, organizations can remain competitive and deliver groundbreaking solutions.
Prompt engineering prioritizes efficiency and efficacy when addressing challenges. By empowering teams to identify

problems, develop solutions, and implement changes swiftly, downtime is reduced, and productivity is maximized.

Organizations can significantly improve customer satisfaction and loyalty through timely solutions. Prompt engineering ensures timely support, updates, and new features for customers, which fosters favourable customer experiences and enduring relationships.

Prompt engineering reduces the time required to introduce new products and features. Organizations can expedite development, reduce constraints, and adopt agile methodologies, enhancing time-to-market performance and maximizing opportunities.

Agility and adaptability are organizational values that are fostered through prompt engineering. As market conditions, customer feedback, and evolving requirements evolve, teams are encouraged to embrace change, iterate swiftly, and pivot as necessary.

Prompt engineering fosters an environment conducive to innovation and experimentation by providing autonomy to investigate novel concepts, validate hypotheses, and undertake calculated risks. Organizations that place a high value on timely engineering are more inclined to foster innovation and maintain a leading position within their respective sectors.

Optimized Resource Utilization: Organizations can reduce waste and maximize resource utilization by prioritizing prompt engineering practices. By identifying inefficiencies, streamlining processes, and allocating resources more efficiently, teams can maximize value delivery and productivity.

Organizations gain a competitive edge in the current fast-paced business environment by implementing prompt engineering. Firms that can promptly and dependably provide solutions of superior quality are more advantageously positioned than their rivals to seize market share.

Employee Satisfaction and Engagement: Prompt engineering enables groups to operate with increased productivity and accomplish significant outcomes through effective collaboration. It is more probable that engaged and content employees will exhibit higher productivity, innovation, and dedication to the organisation's achievement.

Business Resilience: Prompt engineering assists organizations in maintaining their adaptability and resilience during periods of uncertainty and disruption. Organizations can enhance their capacity to overcome obstacles and establish a solid foundation for sustained prosperity by adopting a mindset that values adaptability, capability, and promptness.

In conclusion, in the current dynamic and competitive environment, entities that wish to prosper must prioritize expeditious engineering. Organizations that emphasize speed, agility, and customer focus can accomplish innovation, provide value, and sustain a competitive advantage.

ABOUT THE AUTHOR

Dheeraj Mehrotra, MS, MPhil, PhD (Education Management)., a white and a yellow belt in SIX SIGMA, a Certified NLP Business Diploma holder, is an Educational Innovator, Author, with expertise in Six Sigma In Education, Academic Audits, Neuro-Linguistic Programming (NLP), Total Quality Management In Education, an Experiential Educator, a CBSE Resource towards School Assessment (SQAA), CCE, JIT, Five S, and KAIZEN. He has authored over 100 books on computer science, AI, digital body language, NLP, quality circles, school management, classroom effectiveness, and safety and security. A former Principal at De Indian Public School, New Delhi, (INDIA), NPS International School, Guwahati, and Education Officer at GEMS, Gurgaon, with ample teaching experience of over Three Decades, he is a certified Trainer for Quality Circles/ TQM in Education and QCI Standards for School Accreditation/ School Audits and Management. He has also been honoured with the President of India's National Teacher Award in 2006 and the Best Science Teacher State Award (By the Ministry of Science and Technology, State of UP), Innovation in Education for his inception of Six Sigma In Education by Education Watch, New Delhi and

Education World- Best Teacher Award, BOLT Learner Teacher Award by Air India, 'Innovation in Education Award 2016' by Higher Education Forum (HEF), Gujarat Chapter, among others. He has developed over 150 FREE EDUCATIONAL MOBILE Apps for the Google Play Store exclusively for Teachers, Students, and Parents. This work has been recognised by the LIMCA BOOK OF RECORDS and INDIA BOOK OF RECORDS as the only Indian to draw that feast. As a founder president of the IoT Society of India, he also promotes Technology Globally. Dr Mehrotra is presently engaged as a PRINCIPAL at KUNWARS GLOBAL SCHOOL, Lucknow, India. He has conducted over 2000 workshops globally on "Excellence In Education" integrated with Total Quality Management and Six Sigma, Technology Integration in Education (TIE), Developing towards being ROCKSTAR TEACHERS, including Cyberspace, Cyber Security, Classroom Management, School Leadership & Management, and Innovative teaching within classrooms via Mind Maps, NLP and Experiential Learning in Academics. He is an active TEDx speaker and can be viewed on the YouTube TEDx channel. As a premium UDEMY Instructor, he has developed over 450 courses and caters to over 8 Lakh students from 180 countries. He can be visited at www.authordheerajmehrotra.com

Books By The Same Author

Books

Cyber Security For Kids	Classroom Teaching Ideas	BASICS OF ARTIFICIAL...	Smart Career Planner	Student Engagement...	Marketing Mantras For...
2022	2022	2019	2020	2022	2021

Tools And Tips For Teaching...	Quality Circles in Schools	Basics of Artificial...	Teacher's Toolkit Post...	AI Basics for School...	Basics of Go Programming
2021	2022	2021	2021	2019	2022

Optimising Educational...
2022

High Performance...
2020

Learning Beyond COVID
2022

Secrets to Raising a...
2022

101 SCHOOL MANAGEME...
2017

Digital Body Language
2020

The Quality Icon
2022

Academic Quality...
2022

The One Minute Educator
2021

Digital Wellbeing For...
2022

The 64 Kalas of Krishna For...
2023

Risk Management...
2022

R Programming
For Beginners
2021

Impact of
Information...
2021

Pedagogical
Practices to...
2022

Motivating &
Quality...
2022

Child
Safeguarding ...
2022

Climate
Classroom
2021

NEP 2020- At a
Glance for...
2021

Street Smart
Teaching...
2021

Optimal Child
Development
2022

Roadmap To A
New Normal...
2020

Teaching in a
Digital Age
2022

Conscious
Parenting
2021

School

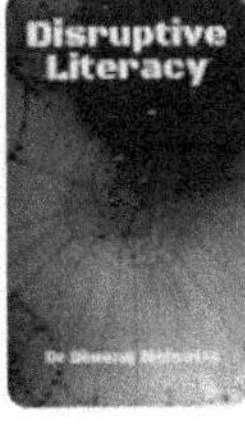

Disruptive

Ways to

100 Ideas For

100 Green

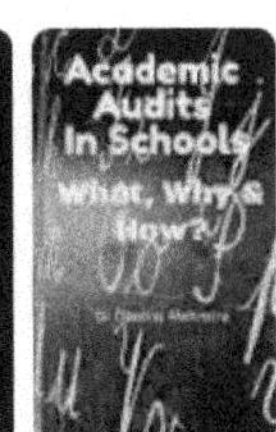

Academic

R Programming For Beginners
2021

Impact of Information…
2021

Pedagogical Practices to…
2022

Motivating & Quality…
2022

Child Safeguarding …
2022

Climate Classroom
2021

NEP 2020- At a Glance for…
2021

Street Smart Teaching…
2021

Optimal Child Development
2022

Roadmap To A New Normal…
2020

Teaching in a Digital Age
2022

Conscious Parenting
2021

School

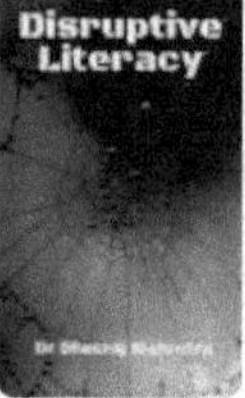

Disruptive

Ways to

100 Ideas For

100 Green

Academic

Human Rights
Education

2021

What & Why? A
Know How…

2020

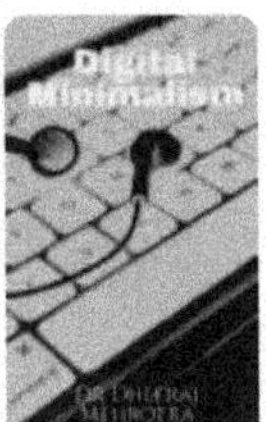

Digital
Minimalism

2022

Teaching in the
Vuca World

2021

Applying SIX
SIGMA Within…

2021

100 Simple
Teaching…

2021

Coding For Kids
in Python

2020

Tools For
Quality For…

2022

Harvesting
Excellence

2021

www.ingramcontent.com/pod-product-compliance
Lightning Source LLC
Chambersburg PA
CBHW040133150726
48005CB00015B/2477